THE BLOOD OF RACHEL

THE BLOOD OF RACHEL

COTTON NOE

ISBN: 978-93-5420-661-0

Published: 1916

© 2021
LECTOR HOUSE LLP

LECTOR HOUSE LLP
E-MAIL: lectorpublishing@gmail.com

"I will not come
At his command. I have a royal heart
And will not thus disgra0e the Persian throne."

THE BLOOD OF RACHEL

A DRAMATIZATION OF ESTHER AND OTHER POEMS

BY

COTTON NOE

Author of "The Loom of Life"

1916

TO
HONORABLE MOSES KAUFMAN

From whom I differ on some political and religious questions,
but whose warm friendship and keen literary appreciation
have been a source of much inspiration to me,
particularly in the writing of this drama.

CONTENTS

POSTSCRIPT

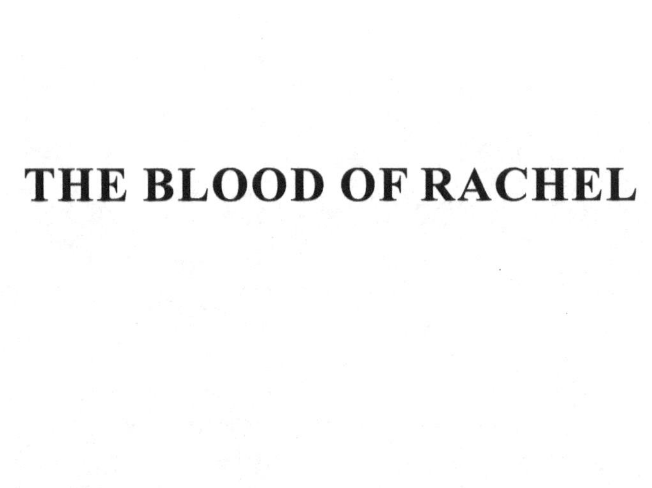

THE BLOOD OF RACHEL

PERSONS OF THE DRAMA

AHASUERUS	King of Persia
VASHTI	Queen of Persia
ESTHER	Second Queen of Persia
HAMAN	Premier
MORDECAI	A Jew, afterwards Premier
ZERESH	Wife of Haman
MEHEUMAN	A Chamberlain
ABAGTHA	Another Chamberlain
AHAFID	Court Poet
SMERDIS	Court Fool
SAADI	Young Court Poet
PARSHANDATHA	Lady in Waiting to Zeresh
ZETHAR	Lady in Waiting to Vashti

Chamberlains, Ladies and Gentlemen of the Court, Heralds, Royal Dancers, Nubian Slaves, Waiters, and others.

ACT I

ACT I

SCENE I

Place—Shushan, the Capital of Persia.

Time—478 B.C.

[*A hall in the palace of the king. Enter Smerdis, the king's jester, and Ahafid, poet and minstrel to the king, from opposite sides of the hall. Ahafid is already an old man, with long grey beard and a little stooped with age. He carries a golden Persian harp on which he plays and accompanies his own song.*]

Ahafid

[*Sings.*]

Now War has doffed his mailed coat
And Peace forgot her art;
The lute but not the bugle's note
Can stir the kingly heart;
Nights of revel and carp,
And days of sensuous rust,
How can a poet's harp
Intone a song of lust?

The king is mad. His flight from Salamis
Was bad enough. But that could be excused.
For six months now what has he done but drink,
Carouse and wallow in lascivious ease,
While subjects driven to despair with tax
Have fallen on the poisoned sword and cursed
In death the son of their once goodly king?

Smerdis

Ahafid, you do seem to think the first
Great business of a king is war. Now pray
You, why should Xerxes waste the lusty days
Of youth in bloody strife? To furnish themes,
No doubt, for dullard bards and minstrelsy.
Ahasuerus is the wisest king

That ever sat upon a Persian throne.
You graybeard fool, stupid as poets are.
Can you not see the wisdom of our king
In substitution of the flight for death,
Of feast for fight, of wine for blood? Think you
'Tis wise to wear the plaited mail of Mars
When Venus bids you to the festival
Of love?

Ahafid

You call me then a graybeard fool!
Though I have dropped the purple bloom of spring
The autumn's silvery down may indicate
The ripened fruit of wisdom which your youth
Has never tasted. Smerdis, you are blind!
My beard is white, but vision clear. The king
Does daily waste the substance of his realm,
And nightly dissipates his energies
In vices of the blood. Vashti, the queen,
The idol of her people, is in grief.

Smerdis

In grief for what? Does she too wish the king
To take the field? I know our queen is fair
Of face and most voluptuous of form.
Perhaps her grief is due to jealousy.
Would she monopolize his love, because
Her beauty is surpassing?

Ahafid

Vashti does
Not know that she is beautiful. She loves
Her country and is brave as well as good.
I dread the issue of this night. The king
Has ordered that the queen be brought before
The court, a target for licentious eyes.
She will refuse to go because her heart
Is pure. Ahasuerus, flushed with wine,
Will brook no opposition to his will.
A tragedy that never Persia knew
Will see the rising of to-morrow's sun.

Smerdis

A tragedy no country ever knew—
A woman who is beautiful, but doesn't know it's true.

Ahafid

[*Sings.*]

Oh, for a song to cleanse the heart
Or touch the sceptred power;
Oh, might the gods a strength impart
To meet this tragic hour.

[*Exeunt Ahafid and Smerdis.*]

[*Enter Vashti and Zethar.*]

Vashti

Oh, Zethar, do you think this night will end
The revels that dishonor Persia's king?
To-day unknown I strolled through squalid parts
Of this old city and observed the poor.
My lord, unmindful of their misery,
Has laid a heavy tax for his insane
Extravagance upon the helpless child
That begs in Shushan's streets. Not here alone,
This suffering; but Persia's peasantry,
The glory of the old empire, the heart
That once defied the world, is broken on
The wheel of tax. And all for what?

Zethar

O queen,
Always the world has had its poverty.
You shall forget the poor. One stoop of wine
Will bring you happiness. Vashti, drink.

Vashti

Forgive me, Zethar, but no wine to-night.

[*Enter Meheuman, Biztha and Abagtha.*]

Meheuman

[*Loftily.*]

Our most imperial queen, the king has laid
A banquet in the palace garden court,
The crowning act of that munificence
Toward prince and people great and small alike,
Ahasuerus now for many months
Has shown the loyal subjects of his realm.
The adornment of the court displays a rich
Magnificence of taste; the couches are

Of fretted gold and silver set upon
A pavement of mosaic inlaid stone.
The drinking is according to the law —
None can compel, each vessel is diverse,
But all of gold. Th' abundance of the wine
Shows the unstinted bounty of the king.
Our monarch's heart is merry in the cup,
And boasts that Vashti's beauty does excel
In magic power the fabled Helen's charms,
And bids us bring immediately before
The court great Persia's matchless queen!

Vashti

Meheuman, tell Ahasuerus I
Must thank his majesty since he can still
Remember Vashti's beauty, though his grace
Has lost all sense of modesty and shame.
You say his heart is merry now in wine
And that he glories with exceeding pride
Because my face is fair to look upon!
I do not doubt his tongue is eloquent;
The fiery phrase is his! Why, often I
Have heard him praise his horse in language that
Seemed kindled at the altar of the gods.
It may be that he holds me higher than
His hundred concubines.

Meheuman

Your majesty,
The king does hold his queen a goddess.

Vashti

Well,
Perhaps he thinks himself divine. Go tell
The king I do not wish to be enrolled
Among divinities. I am the queen —
He must respect me as the one who wears
The Persian crown.

'Tis scarce three years since he
Began to reign. He was Darius' son —
A king of whom the world was proud. He wooed
Me as a prince of noble blood, and I
Received his hand with dignity as well
As love. I was a princess, but I had
A heart. Long since I found that he had none.

A hundred eighty days continuous feast
He has oppressed the people of his rule
With drunken revels and with wanton waste.
And now to crown his sensuality
He sends his vulgar chamberlains to bring
Me to his palace garden that his lords
May gaze with unchaste eyes upon my form.
Meheuman, Biztha, will you tell the king
That Vashti bids him come to her if he
Would see the queen.

Meheuman

You understand
The costly hangings of the garden court
Are blue and green and white?

Vashti

Now pray you what
Significance has that? What if each couch
Is gold and silver and each goblet set
With stones?

Meheuman

The king's great love for Vashti!

Vashti

Then
He has prepared this banquet for his queen?
And does he think this is an evidence
Of love. It rather means the king's debauched.
I will not be a party to his sin.

Meheuman

The etiquette of court commands you to
Obey.

Vashti

Commands! Well, has it come to that?
But I will not obey. I am a queen!
Here! Take this purple robe and coronet,
And tell Ahasuerus to adorn
Some harlot of his harem. She will grace
The queenship of his kingdom better than
A pure and modest wife.

Abagtha

You do not know
The meaning of your words!

Vashti

Abagtha, why
Do you admonish me? Do I not know
The forfeit? Chamberlains, this message take
Licentious Xerxes from his virtuous queen:
I do not fear his wrath. I will not come
At his command. I have a royal heart
And will not thus disgrace the Persian throne.
The king that's halfway worthy of my hand
Would hate the queen that yielded to his lust.
My heart, O chamberlains, is broken, not
That Vashti's crown is lost, but oh, to see
The regal name of Persia brought so low!
I weep. The tears are for my country. Go!

[*Exeunt Vashti, Abagtha, etc.*]

[*Curtain is lowered to denote the passage of six years.*]

SCENE II

[Outer hall in palace. Throne room back concealed by curtain. Queen Esther, disguised by loose dress thrown over royal robe and head and face below the eyes hidden by mask, approaches the door where Mordecai, the Jew, is standing.]

Mordecai

Ah, Esther! Though your queenly robe you do
Conceal, I know that regal gait. Before
I ever looked upon these palace walls,
When you were yet a little child beyond
The purple peaks, where shepherds led their flocks
In pastures green, I often dreamed that you
Would one day wear a golden coronet
And sit in majesty upon a throne.

Esther

[Dejectedly.]

Four years I have been queen, which time I have
Not heard the voice of any one I love;
And though disguised, I hardly dare to speak
My heart even to you. This palace is
A gloomy prison cell. The Persian crown
Is meaningless to me. The hundred gems
That blaze upon its field of gold are dull
And heavy lead. I would exchange it all
For but a glint of sunshine on the hills
Where I was born. But why this interview?

Mordecai

My royal niece, I know that you are queen.

Esther

A queen? But what of that? Though of my blood,
You can not even look upon my face.
What would you have?

[Wailing without.]

Mordecai

My daughter, do you hear
The cries of anguish that disturb the peace
Of Shushan's streets? Your people everywhere
Are clothed in sackcloth. Read the king's decree!

[*Handing her paper.*]

Esther

[*Reads.*]

"It has been written and commanded by
Ahasuerus, emperor of all
The East, and sealed in every tongue with his
Own ring—the royal seal—that governors
And princes and lieutenants, everyone
Within the Persian rule, shall make and cause
To die and perish every Jew, both young
And old, the women and the children, rich
And poor alike, and forfeit all their goods.
This is Ahasuerus' sovereign will
And shall be done and executed in
The month of Adar on the thirteenth day."
Oh, God! It is Ahasuerus' seal.

Mordecai

But Haman's hand.

Esther

Why does the premier hate
The Jews?

Mordecai

Because the children of the true
And living God will never bend the knee
To heathen pride. He hates the Jews because
Your uncle is a child of Abraham
And will not do obeisance to a son
Of Baal. Esther, though I made you queen,
I plead not for the life of Mordecai,
But for the sacred blood of Israel.
You alone can intervene. Go straight
Before the king and make demand that he
Reverse this law that puts the Jews to death.

Esther

A Persian king can not reverse his own
Decree. Besides, the queen who goes into
The presence of her lord unless by his
Express command, must sacrifice her life,
Except through some unguarded impulse he
Extends his golden sceptre that she live.
I can not go unto the king.

Mordecai

Your life
Is forfeited already, child; you are
A Jew.

Esther

You did conceal my blood nor dare
Reveal my lineage now. Your own deceit
Has brought this death upon the house of Israel,
Nor will Jehovah hold you guiltless in
The hour of doom.

Mordecai

Esther, if you keep
Your peace when Rachel's children wail and cry
For help, deliverance will arise
Unto the Jews but you shall be destroyed
And all your father's house.

Esther

Depart. [*Sound of trumpets within.*]
The king
Is on his throne. I go, and if I die,
I can but perish. Peace to Israel.

[*Exit Mordecai.*]

[*The curtain back rises and discloses Ahasuerus on his throne surrounded by court.
Esther approaches to center of hall before the king, and extends her hands as though sup-
plicating. The king seems dazed for a moment and then deeply moved; slowly he lifts the
golden sceptre and extends it toward the queen who approaches and touches it.*]

Ahasuerus

Why did you, Esther, O most beauteous queen,
Thus dare to come unbidden to the king?
'Twas jealous Death unbarred the royal door

That he might claim you for his paramour?
Your innocence and charms have saved your life!

Esther

[*Innocently.*]

My lord, how now was I in danger? Ah,
You know I am your loyal wife? I would
Not be your queen alone. The crown is naught
Compared to pleasures of companionship.
O Xerxes, may not Esther share your joys
Of wine and song? Too long you have denied
That which I covet most—to be beside
My king.

Ahasuerus

There is no favor, Esther, I
Would longer hold from you; even to half
My kingdom, tell me what you most desire,
And I will give it you.

Esther

My lord, I have
Already spoke my heart, but you will not
Believe. To test Ahasuerus' love,
I have a favor I would ask of you;
But first that.my most gracious lord may know
His queen has taste and skill as well as charms,
I will prepare a banquet for the king
With my own hands. You are a judge of wine,
And every dish that graces banquet halls.
To-morrow, let Ahasuerus come,
And bring his premier Haman, who no doubt
Can tell a heron from a hawk, and if
My lord shall praise my art, and I
Find favor in his sight, I will make known
My dearest wish.

Ahasuerus

Oh, Esther, you have pleased
Your king already far beyond what he
Had ever hoped. To-morrow night at six!

[*Music and revels. Esther retires.*]

[*The king and retinue retire in opposite direction. Haman and followers pass out front
where Mordecai sits by the gate, together with others. All except Mordecai salaam, but the*

Jew remains stiff, looking Haman defiantly in the face.]

[*Curtain.*]

SCENE III

Home of Haman—two days later.

[Enter Haman, Zeresh, and Parshandatha.]

Haman

My star grows brighter with each setting sun;
The lowly child of old Hammedetha
Is first among the servants of the king.
Ah, Mordecai, you did not know I am
An Agagite, who fed upon the breast
Of unrelenting hate toward every child
Of Israel, who will not bend the knee
Save to the God of Abraham. Oh, do.

[Wailing in Street.]

You, Zeresh, hear that wail of anguish? Love,
I know that you are proud to be the wife
Of him who can direct such music.

Zeresh

I
Am proud of Haman's power.

Haman

Go call our friends.

Zeresh

Before the rising sun had touched with gold
The treetops on the peaks of Zagros, Tesh,
The son of Zalphon, was abroad
In Shushan on the errand of my lord.

Haman

Not only in this city, but, my spouse,
In every province of the king, the Jews
In sackcloth mourn because of Haman's might.
But would you know the secret of my strength?

This ring! The seal of Xerxes. It is death
To every drop of Jacob's blood within
The Domain of Ahasuerus' rule.

Zeresh

The guests are coming.

Haman

Oh, the messages
Of enmity are swift as shafts of love.
Now, Zeresh, call the servants of the house
And set a sumptuous feast, for Haman would
Take counsel of his friends.

Zeresh

My gracious lord,
The table is already set. Go greet
The guests and bring them in.

[Exit Haman.]

[Zeresh continues.]

Parshandatha,
What do you think of Haman? Did you note
My lord?

Parshandatha

I did, madam. His happiness
Is most complete. His rapid rise to power
Has all but ravished him with joy. And yet,
Methought that something still he lacked. Perhaps
The queen's consent has not yet been obtained
To this decree that puts the Jews to death.

Zeresh

What do you mean? The queen's consent? My Lord
Has naught to do with Xerxes' wife, and why
Should he be troubled for a woman's whim?
Besides, who knows but Esther does approve
This slaughter of the Jews?

Parshandatha

Approve, madam?
She is a queen, but still a woman!

Zeresh

So
Am I, though not a queen! A woman, yes
But with no stomach for that hated race!

Parshandatha

'Tis whispered in the court that Esther is
Herself a Jew.

Zeresh

The Persian queen a Jew!
Then let her perish with her blood.

Parshandatha

But would
My lord consent to Esther's death?

Zeresh

Consent
Again! Parshandatha, why do you harp
Upon consent? Now listen to my words.
But should you e'er disclose one breath
Of what I say, you are yourself a Jew,
Nor is there any power in Persia's king
To save your life. My lord pretends to hate
The Jews. His hate is only wounded pride.
The deference of Mordecai is all
That Haman wants. He does not know the queen
Is Hebrew blood. This fact must still be kept
Concealed—concealed, that is, until the day
Of death. Oh, he shall know who Esther is—
This Israelite that banquets with my lord!
You think his rise is due to Esther's power?

Parshandatha

Madam, I do not know.

Zeresh

Not know! not know!
But what think you, Parshandatha? Of course
You do not know.

Parshandatha

Madam, he often dines

With Esther and the king. The king no doubt
Is very fond of your most gracious lord.

Zeresh

The king!

Parshandatha

Mayhap the queen also. Your lord
Is young and handsome still. The king is far
Beyond the queen in years.

Zeresh

I can
Not catch your drift.

Parshandatha

Madam, your husband has
A ready wit. The queen enjoys life.

Zeresh

Enjoys life!
And so do I, and likewise death. Now hold
Your blasted tongue. My husband sups again
To-morrow with the Jewish queen. They say
When Haman dines her majesty prepares
The banquet with her own most dainty hand!
Parshandatha, whose hand, think you, has laid
The feast of Adar?

Parshandatha

Zeresh! call you death
A feast!

Zeresh

A glorious feast on which my soul
Already feeds, and Esther shall be there!

[*Re-enter Haman and Friends.*]

Haman

Be seated at the table.
Citizens
Of Shushan, patriots of Persia, friends,
The servant of the king has called you here

To tell you of his triumph and to ask
Your sage advice. Two days ago the prince
And I sat down together to a feast
Within the palace walls and drank your health.
The royal cup was blushing like the spume
Of autumn clouds at sunset, when a wail
Arose in Shushan that has sore perplexed
The people. Mordecai, the haughty Jew,
Who sits beside the palace gate, refused
To bow or do me reverence, although
Admonished by the king. I was born
A humble subject in the private ranks
Of life; but now I wear the signet ring
Of Xerxes. Friends, the law that dooms the Jews
To simultaneous slaughter can not be
Revoked. Last night the queen invited me
To banquet with her lord. The necklace that
She wore of iridescent pearls was like
A rainbow over polar snows. Ah, she
Was fair to look upon! And now my cup
Was filled to overflowing—

[*Zeresh shows great emotion.*]

(Zeresh, are
You ill?)—when Esther begged that I would come
Again to-morrow to another feast
Her hand would lay for Haman and the king.
My wealth is multiplied beyond my ken;
The sceptre is almost within my grasp.
But all these things avail me naught, so long
As yonder hated Jew remains unbent.

A Friend

Destroy the brute at once!

Haman

Oh, that will not
Suffice. 'Tis not his death, but homage that
Must sweeten my revenge. Ah, I would see
Him groveling on the earth as Haman passed.
My rank and station must be recognized.
I sit beside the king; I am premier
Of Persia. Yet this Jewish dog is still
Unmoved!

Zeresh

Hang him where the kites will eat
His eyes!

Haman

O Zeresh, you are like the rising sun—
An inspiration in the hour of gloom.
We'll build this gallows fifty cubits high,
And then his Hebrew pride will bite the dust.
Oh, I can hear him whining like a cur,
My love, your wisdom is above the head.
A woman's heart is like an oracle
Divine. Prepare this gallows. Friends, I go
At dawn to greet the king. At night we dine
Alone with Esther, and—

[*Zeresh faints.*]

Why Zeresh, are
You ill again? Send for the leech. Her blood
Is over wrought with too much happiness.

[*Curtain.*]

ACT II

ACT II

SCENE I

Place—The palace of the king. Outer room of banquet hall. Curtain back.

[Enter Meheuman, Biztha, and Smerdis.]

Meheuman

Ahafid has become most deaf of late;
Advancing age has wrought a piteous change
In him. He can not understand our king.

Smerdis

'Tis not the king but age that makes him groan.
I mean this age, the age in which we live.

> *[Meheuman and Biztha exeunt on the opposite side of*
> *stage, as Ahafid enters more stooped, and singing.]*

Ahafid

[Sings.]

A country but no king,
An empire but no throne,
An upstart wears the signet ring,
My harp has lost its tone.
I can no longer sing great Persia's praise.

Smerdis

The trouble isn't with the harp, the country, king, nor throne;
Nor that an upstart wears the ring: Ahafid's voice is gone.

Ahafid

What say you, Smerdis?

Smerdis

Art is marvelous.

Ahafid

Even Ahasuerus once was king,
He was a despot, it is true, but still
A prince.

Smerdis

If prince, then why not still a king?

Ahafid

Eh, Smerdis?

Smerdis

[*Aloud.*]

More than prince and less than king.

Ahafid

Why now the sceptre, aye, almost the crown
Are worn by Haman, not of noble birth,
But lowborn, vulgar, raised by royal will
To first place in a land renowned for blood.

Smerdis

To first place in a land renowned for fools.

Ahafid

What's that?

Smerdis

This Haman is a cunning fox.

Ahafid

The exile of the virtuous Vashti was
A fatal sin.

Smerdis

She should have feasted with
The king.

Ahafid

I did not hear.

Smerdis

[*Aloud.*]

Old Xerxes lost
The finest houri in his harem. Oh,
The royal fool!

Ahafid

The Jewess Esther's but
A girl, as beauteous as a lustrous star,
But innocent as dawn of dew-washed day.

Smerdis

As wise as snakes and innocent as doves!

Ahafid

What, Smerdis, what? You catch my simile?

Smerdis

Ah, yes, Ahafid, yes, Aurora in
The bath pool. That was fine. Your poetry
Like wine improves with age. Go on, go on,
Let's have another picture of the dawn.

Ahafid

Her beauty made her queen, but can not save
Her life.

Smerdis

Ahasuerus will attend
To that.

Ahafid

[*Not hearing.*] Ahasuerus does not seem
To know a Persian law can not be changed.

Smerdis

He knows that lawyers can be bribed.

Ahafid

What's that?

Smerdis

[*Louder.*]

Just thinking of the lustrous stars of dawn.

Ahafid

But Mordecai believes that Esther can
Control the king, and yet may save the Jews.

Smerdis

I am more interested in fools than Jews.

Ahafid

The golden sceptre was extended when
She went into his presence yesterday.
Last night she banqueted with him but still
Refused to name the favor that she wished.

Smerdis

A bathrobe or some new stars for her crown.

Ahafid

[*Not hearing.*]

The king does not suspect her origin.
What will he do when he finds out the truth?

Smerdis

Since when has Xerxes cared for truth?

Ahafid

What say?

Smerdis

He'll add two extra stars to Esther's crown.

Ahafid

Beloved Vashti lives in poverty,
The victim of a lewd and brutal whim.
And now it seems that Esther's fate was sealed
When Haman wrote that every Jew must die
Because the Hebrew Mordecai refused
Obeisance to his over-bearing pride.

Smerdis

Watch Esther smash that seal.

Ahafid

I did not hear.

Smerdis

[*Louder.*]

Still quoting lines upon the innocence
Of lustrous stars, and dawn of dew-washed day.

Ahafid

[*Singing.*]

Minstrelsy shall be no more,
The poet's tongue is still;
The strings that woke to deeds of yore
No longer feel the thrill.

Smerdis

I'm glad no more we'll feel the thrill
For I, for one have had my fill.

Ahafid

Eh, Smerdis?

Smerdis

[*Louder.*]

Bathing in that simile.

[*Exeunt Ahafid and Smerdis.*]

SCENE II

[The curtain rises, disclosing Ahasuerus, Esther, Haman, and attendants at the banquet table.]

Ahasuerus

Beloved Esther, my most beauteous queen,
This banquet does surpass in excellence
Even the feast of yesterday, which you
Prepared for Haman and the king. Your hand
Grows deft with practice.

Esther

But, my lord, you are
A connoisseur, and can but speak these words
In flattery. O king, it was my heart,
And not my hand that flavored every dish
That lies before you.

Ahasuerus

Esther, now it is
Your tongue that flatters. Still, it does rejoice
Me much to hear such language from the queen.
A connoisseur, say you? Haman, can
You tell me, now, what bay or bight in all
The salted seas once held this shrimp?

[Holding up shrimp.]

Haman

[Tasting it meditatively.]

My lord,
I think it must have been the Persian Gulf.

Ahasuerus

Ha, ha, Haman, why you do not know
A wild goose from the Bird of Paradise.
This crangonoid is found nowhere except

Along the Red Sea beach not far from where
The hosts of Pharaoh were engulfed and lost.

Esther

[*With suppressed emotion.*]

Oh, king, your tongue is most acute. But whence,
Think you, this tinct of cinnamon that makes
The savor of the dish.

Ahasuerus

[*Tasting for a long time.*]

I give it up,
Unless it came from Java or Ceylon.

Esther

[*Laughing, changing rapidly to deep feeling.*]

My lord, it is not cinnamon at all,
But spice that grew a thousand years ago
In hills beyond the Jordon. Haman, can
You tell the flavor of the grape that fills
Your goblet?

Haman

[*Flattered.*]

Oh, I think it must have grown
In islands of the blue Aegean Sea.

Esther

[*Turning to the king.*]

My lord, it is the selfsame cup they drank
From sacred vessels at Belshazzar's feast
That night in Babylon.

Haman

What means the queen,
This wine is not that old, and yet, 'tis not
Excelled at banquets of the gods.

Ahasuerus

[*Showing effect of wine.*]

Nor kings.
This is a joyous night! Oh, queen, your wit

Has filled my cup with wine of happiness.
What think you, Haman, should be done to him
The king delighteth most to honor now?

Haman

Bring forth the robe, O king, your majesty
Does wear, and place it on the one your grace
Does most delight to honor. Xerxes, set
This man upon your royal horse, and place
Your majesty's own jeweled crown upon
His head, and let him be proclaimed
Throughout the public streets.

Ahasuerus

[*Rises. Emphatic.*]

So let it then
Be done to Mordecai, the Jew beside
The palace gate.

Haman

What words are these?
You can not mean the Jew!

Ahasuerus

[*More emphatic.*]

The Jew I mean.
Last night I could not sleep, and so I had
The book of records read, the chronicles,
Wherein I learned that this same Mordecai
The Jew had saved Ahasuerus' life,
When Teresh and another chamberlain
Had sought to lay the hand of violence
Upon your king. Let nothing fail of all
That you have spoken should be done to him
The king delighteth now to honor most.
And Esther, tell Ahasuerus now
Your dearest wish. On yesterday I begged
To know the favor you did most desire
And now it shall be granted unto you,
Whatever your request, even to half
My kingdom, it shall be performed.

Esther

[*With hands extended toward the king.*]

Have I
Found favor in your sight, O king, then let
My life be given unto me at my
Petition and my people live at my
Request! For we are sold to be destroyed—
To perish and be slain.

Ahasuerus

[*Surprised and dazed.*]

O where is he—
Oh, who is he, that dare presume to lay
The hand of violence upon my queen!

Esther

There stands this adversary, O my king,
The wicked Haman!

Ahasuerus

Haman! Haman! What
Can be the meaning of this speech? This man
I have advanced to be my premier?

Esther

I mean this craven whom you have advanced
To put to death with your own royal seal
The queen, as well as every other Jew
That breathes the Persian air, both young and old
Alike, the laughing child and gray-haired sire.

Ahasuerus

What! Esther, you a Jew!

Esther

[*Proudly.*]

I am a Jew.
A daughter of the tribe of Benjamin—
Pure Hebrew blood!

[*A dramatic pause. Esther awaits the decision of the king, who for a time seems to waver, then extends his sceptre toward Esther. Harbonah, the king's high officer, appears. Haman throws himself at Esther's feet.*]

Haman

[*Pleading.*]

Oh, queen, I do beseech
You, save me from his wrath.

Ahasuerus

[*Angrily.*]

Harbonah, let
This traitor, Haman, die at once.

Harbonah

My lord,
You know the scaffold that the premier built
For Mordecai?

Ahasuerus

The premier! What's that,
Harbonah? You mock your king? Let him
Be hanged upon this gallows. Call the Jew!
He holds the first place in my kingdom now.

[*Exeunt Ahasuerus, Esther, Haman, Harbonah, and attendants.*]

Zeresh

[*Who has been concealed in a corner of the hall, advancing.*]

At Esther's feet! An Aggagite! Ha, Ha!
A hater of the Jews! You hypocrite!
A lover of this queen! A paramour
Of her who boasts that she can trace her blood
An unpolluted stream a thousand years
To one who watched his humble flocks on bleak
Judean hills. A shepherd queen that rules
The Persian throne, and you, O Haman, you
That fed on venom for her race, are now,
Though premier, a cringing, craven wretch,
Begging this Jewish girl for worthless life.
"A rainbow over polar snows," ha, ha!
No doubt her grace was fair to look upon.
False-hearted queen, O royal prostitute!
It was your jeweled hand that laid this feast
But Zeresh's heart that furnished all the wine!

[*Curtain.*]

ACT III

ACT III

SCENE I

Some time Later. Room in the Palace of Shushan.

[Enter Ahafid and Smerdis.]

Ahafid

[Singing.]

In the morning man may flourish
In the evening be cut down;
Dawn may find a hero famous,
Nightfall see him lose renown.

Smerdis

[Singing.]

In his youth Ahafid's singing
Was the pride of Persia's rule;
Now that age has come upon him,
Hear him braying like a mule.

Ahafid

Still singing like a nightingale, say you?

Smerdis

[Aloud.]

I did. [*Aside*] The long-eared kind that crops the grass.

Ahafid

Haman's hanged upon the scaffold that
He built for Mordecai. The Jew now wears
The signet ring that sealed his nation's life.
His nation's life? But how can he explain
The slaughter of the Persian hosts?

Smerdis

Now if he would, I think he could, and if he should,
He'd thus explain: "The hosts were slain because my brain
Was not insane. So I raised Cain, obtained the reign
Of this campaign, and still remain, though they were slain."

Ahafid

I think I must be growing deaf. You rhymed?

Smerdis

I only spoke a little joke. If I could sing, I'd say the ring,
And not the king explains the thing.

Ahafid

But does
The God of Abraham inspire revenge?
The worshippers of Moloch would have shrunk
From such a day of death. I marvel that
Queen Esther did not intervene. She rules
The king. But wherefore did I say the king?

Smerdis

I think it must have been to rhyme with ring.

Ahafid

Darius' son's a spineless debauchee.

[*Sings.*]

The Jew the purple robe enfolds
And eke the royal gown;
For Mordecai the sceptre holds
And Esther wears the crown.

[*Exit Ahafid.*]

Smerdis

Ahafid said he couldn't sing Ahasuerus' praise,
And that his harp had lost the tone it had in other days.
But though the Jews are on the throne and Xerxes maudlin full,
Ahafid once more tunes his lyre and bellows like a bull.

Look out, here comes the Jew, a cloud upon
His brow, the weight of empires on his brain.
What matters does he now revolve? I fear
The day of Adar troubles Mordecai.

We'll stand aside and hear the premier.

[Exit Smerdis.]

[Enter Mordecai meditatively, followed by Zeresh, who is unseen by him at first.]

Mordecai

The name of Haman perish from the earth!
The seed of Abraham be multiplied
Until they are as numberless as sands
Upon ocean's shore! This was my prayer,
I learned it at my mother's knee. Was I
Not justified?

Zeresh

[Disguised as a Hebrew woman.]

The Holy Scripture saith,
"Vengeance belongs to God."

Mordecai

But was I not
His instrument? Jehovah wrought through me;
His will, not mine was done.

Zeresh

And yet His will
Was yours?

Mordecai

The wicked Haman would have slain
Even the queen herself and every Jew
That lives within the hundred provinces
Of Xerxes' weak and vacillating rule.

Zeresh

Thy action was no more than self-defense?

Mordecai

Not self-defense of Mordecai alone,
But of my blood, of Esther and the sons
Of Jacob, exiled and defenseless else.
The God of Abraham may chasten, but
He keeps his promises, nor will forsake.
Rameses sat upon his haughty throne

And knew not Joseph, for my people were
Oppressed with bitter bondage and their lives
Made hard in mortar and in brick; but still
They grew in numbers and increased and waxed
Exceeding mighty, till the land was filled
With them. And then the king was sore afraid
And wroth because the Jews had never bent
The knee at Egypt's shrines. He could enslave
But not corrupt the children of the true
And living God. And then he called
The Hebrew midwives and commanded them
To slay thereafter every son that might
Be born to Jacob's sacred blood. God kept
His covenant with Abraham and raised
Up Moses, the deliverer, and when
The plagues had failed to soften Pharaoh's heart,
The Lord smote every firstborn in the land
Of Egypt, save where hyssop mixed with blood
Was sprinkled on the lintel of the door
And on the two side posts, as Moses had
Directed. Saviour of his people, son
Of Amram and of Jochebed, obscure
Levites, found in an ark of bulrushes
Afloat among the flags near by the spot
Where Pharaoh's daughter bathed, and yet, and yet—

Zeresh

Was Moses not selected by the Lord
To lead the Israelites into the Land
Of Promise?

Mordecai

[*As in soliloquy.*]

And did he not talk with God
Upon the Mount of Sinai, when smoke
Enveloped all the peak, and even priests
Were not allowed upon that holy ground?
Was I more lowly than was Amram's child?

Zeresh

Yet God exalted him until the throne
Of Egypt was within his grasp.

Mordecai

Though I,

Like Jesse's son, was once a shepherd's lad,
To-day I rule ten million souls.
Now Moses was a vessel of the Lord
When Death passed over every Hebrew home,
But slew the firstborn where no blood was found.
Was this revenge? Not Moses' hand, but God's
Was red.

Zeresh

The servant must obey his Lord.

Mordecai

I did not plot the Persians' death. The plan
Of God was in it all.

Zeresh

Else why were you
Made premier at the moment when the Jews
Faced death in every province of the king?

Mordecai

It was my hand that stopped the massacre,
But God avenged the awful wrong!

Zeresh

And Esther! How is it with her? You made
Her queen. She was a humble Hebrew girl,
Unknown and friendless, but for Mordecai.

Mordecai

She should be grateful for the crown I gave.

Zeresh

But Hatach says her cheeks are often wet
With tears.

Mordecai

It may be that she weeps for him
Who won her girlish heart before we came
To Shushan or had ever seen the king.

Zeresh

And yet that can not be. The shepherd's crook

Is not the golden sceptre of a king.
I have no doubt that she has long since ceased
To think of youthful dreams. She rules the king,
And what more does a woman want?

Mordecai

I did
Not hope to make her understand at once.
My reasons were too subtle for her heart.
And so I kept my counsel, for I knew
No girl would ever sacrifice her love
To save the remnant of a nation's life.

Zeresh

[*Justifying.*]

And why might even Esther not forget
When once she felt the spell of royal power—
The tinsel show and glamour of the court?
No woman lives that would not be a queen.

Mordecai

I knew Ahasuerus was a brute,
But what of that? Through Esther I have saved
A half a million souls.

Zeresh

[*Aside.*]

Through Esther you
Have slain a million souls.

Mordecai

When Jepthah vowed
A vow unto the Lord he kept his pledge
And slew the only daughter of his flesh
For a burnt offering unto God, because
The Ammonites, his enemy, had been
Delivered to the hands of Israel.
Now Esther was my only child.

Zeresh

[*A little sarcastically.*]

You have
Not sacrificed, but elevated her.

Although she does not understand your heart,
She can but bless her uncle Mordecai.

Mordecai

But why should Esther weep? She risked her life
At my behest, but did she not obtain
Great favor with the king?

Zeresh

And Esther's life
Was forfeit then through Haman's wicked hate.

Mordecai

I wear the royal robe of blue and white.

Zeresh

Does Esther think because her vanity
Is flattered by the jewels of a queen
That Mordecai is moved by pomp and show?

Mordecai

'Tis not the kingly trappings but the seal—
Not sceptre merely but the signet ring,
Not rank, but rule that Mordecai would have.
I can not understand her tears no more
Than she knows why I wear the crown. But I
Am justified. Jehovah wrought through me.

[*Exit Mordecai.*]

Zeresh

[*Bursting into fury.*]

Jehovah wrought through him! Hell wrought through him!
I marvel that his tongue is not consumed
By blasted lies. Wait till he feels the flame
That rages in my heart. Hell may not burn
A Jew, but even he can not withstand
The simoon of a fiery dragon's breath!

Parshandatha

But Zeresh, was the Jew not justified?

Zeresh

Justified! gratified! satisfied! Parshandatha,

Justified in Jepthah; gratified
That he is like the meek and lowly son
Of Amram; satisfied that now the crown
Of Persia presses only Hebrew brows.

Parshandatha

[*Sarcastically.*]

You do forget my lord, Darius' son.
You can not think the blood of Jacob flows
Through Xerxes' veins? Does he not wear the crown?

Zeresh

[*With contempt.*]

Ahasuerus wears a pigeon's heart.
The Persian robe's a Jewish gabardine;
The crown, a Hebrew priest's phylactery.
But did you say forget? Have you been so
Long with me, dear, and doubt my memory?
Forget Ahasuerus, did you say?
That minion of a Jewish girl, who sealed
The death of Haman and his sons? His face
Is seared upon my heart, his image burnt
Into my brain. I tell you Xerxes is
No longer king.

Parshandatha

But is not Esther queen?

Zeresh

Parshandatha, why do you taunt me thus?
Have I not proved your friend? Do I deserve
Your mockery?

Parshandatha

I do but speak to sting
You to revenge.

Zeresh

Let fly your venom then.
The Persian empire is in arms. To-night
The king does hold a great carouse. The Jew
Will sit in state beside the profligate.
This blade I have prepared against that hour.
The queen, I understand, will be a blaze

Of gems. Ahasuerus boasts this night
Would all but wreck a petty kingdom.

Parshandatha

He
Should never live to see the rising sun.

Zeresh

The rising sun! My dear, he shall not see
The Pleiades again, and they are up
At nine. When cornet and the trumpet bruit
The entry of the queen, a hundred blades
Like this [*disclosing dagger*] shall be unsheathed.
Parshandatha,
You know whose blood my blade shall drink!
My hour has come! Ah, Esther, you shall sup
Once more with Haman and your drunken lord,
While Zeresh keeps her lonely watch
Beneath the silent, glittering stars. Come on!

[*Exeunt Zeresh and Parshandatha.*]

[*Curtain.*]

SCENE II

Place—Outer hall to throne room, curtain back.

Time—The following evening.

[*Enter Vashti and Esther from opposite sides of the stage.*]

Esther

Ah, here already, Vashti, at my poor
Request, who dared defy a despot king's
Command to come before him and his lords?
Your beauty, radiant and spotless, grows
Each hour of exiled life more potent still
Than when it hurled an oriental crown,
With all its flashing jewels, in the face
Of brutal Xerxes rather than unveil
Unto a drunken court of lustful eyes.
Uncrowned, deposed, you are, yet thrice a queen!

Vashti

The sting, the sting of your envenomed words!

Esther

Forgive me, dear, I do not mock your fate;
No word of mine is spoke in scorn. I would
Exchange the royal robe and crown I wear
For just one hour of virtuous freedom that
Belongs to you.

Vashti

I can not understand!

Esther

I know; 'tis my misfortune, and I called
You to the palace that I might explain.
Yet every word seems cruel mockery.
I do not blame you that your cheek, as chaste
As lilies, blushes at my seeming shame.

Yet, Vashti, can you not believe I need
Your sympathy? I crave your high respect?

Vashti

You must an explanation.

Esther

Well, did you
Not sacrifice a queenship for the gem
That every woman holds above a throne?
How can we estimate your loss? The pomp
That follows majesty; the crooking knee;
Ten thousand minions at your beck and call;
A thousand sycophantic, fawning lords;
A hundred gleaming jeweled chandeliers;
The radiance and rich magnificence
Of court; long hours of revel and of wine;
And then above the splendor and the show
God's finger writing on the wall! Is this
The precious price that you have paid?

Vashti

This is
The price.

Esther

Sweet friend, I thank you. Yes, your loss
Has been my gain! Yet what reward have I?
How I do hate the crown that you did spurn!
O how I love the pearl of greatest price!
God pardon my great sin!

Vashti, I am
A daughter of Rebecca and the blood
Of Rachel pulses in my veins! Beyond
The northern hills, within a valley green,
A shepherd watches o'er his flocks to-night
Beside a starlit stream, and dreams of her
Who gave the promise of her hand when life
Was young and all the earth was pure and fair.

His love was constant as the northern star,
And mine was like the needle pointing true.
That day is but a sad remembrance now.
I never knew the ones who gave me life.
My uncle, Mordecai, who sits in state

Beside the king instructed me in love
And knowledge of my people. Every night,
As well as every day, like Daniel, I
Was taught to pray, my window open toward
Jerusalem. God softened Cyrus' heart
Because of Daniel's prayer. But, Vashti, you
Must know from Persian Gulf to Caspian Sea,
The sons of Jacob still in exile groan
Beneath a tyrant's yoke. I hear the wail
Of Rachel weeping for her children still;
I hear my lover playing on his flute,
Who waits the coming of a faithless bride!
But Mordecai has stayed the hand of Death!

Vashti

And you did eat your heart to save your blood?

Esther

You comprehend at last? Your sympathy,
O Vashti, I must have, if not respect,
Else can I not return unto the king. [*Vashti weeps.*]
There, there, I thank you, sister, friend, proud queen!
The tears that glitter on your cheeks are worth
A diadem of sparkling Indian stones.
But weep no more—your hand—for Esther's heart
Can now endure, since Vashti understands!
The stars are twinkling in the northern skies;
They shimmer on the stream beyond the hills;
The shepherd's reed is wailing on the breeze;
The revels in the palace now begin;
The call has come; I must no longer stay.
The daughter of a Benjamite will lay
Her heart upon the altar of her blood.
Hear you the crimson riot in my veins?
'Tis Rachel's voice! I would that you could know!

....

Forgive me, Vashti, for my brain's distraught!

The lights die out beyond the palace walls.
The stars are hid.... I can no longer hear
The wailing flute.... Return unto your hut.
Ahasuerus calls with mantling wine.
My place is yonder by the king. I go!

[*Exeunt Esther and Vashti.*]

[Enter Ahafid and Smerdis.]

Ahafid

The last word has been spoken
The last true song been sung;
My country's heart is broken,
The poet's harp unstrung.

Smerdis

Ahafid seems to harp upon his strings.

Ahafid

It seems Ahasuerus means to drink
The cup of revel to its bitter lees.

Smerdis

The deeper in the cup he goes
The sweeter is the wine that flows;
The closer to the lees, he thinks,
The purer is the wine he drinks.

Ahafid

Messengers from every province bring
Reports of mutterings and dangerous
Revolt. But Xerxes, heedless still, declares
This night shall dim the glories of the past.

Smerdis

[Sings.]

The lower in the lamp the oil
The fewer are the days of toil.
The brighter burns the wick of life,
The sooner end the days of strife.
'Tis not for oil that Xerxes cares,
But brilliancy of flame that flares.

Ahafid

I hate the Hebrews and their Jewish God;
I hate Jehovah for his jealous love,
But Mordecai refuses to attend
The feast. The God of Israel must save
Us now, or Persia perish utterly.

My hand will pen no ribald verse

This revel to adorn;
Ye gods, inspire my tongue to curse
The day the king was born.

[Exit Ahafid.]

Smerdis

The more he swears the less he sings,
Then welcome is this news he brings;
For listening to his song is worse
Than hearing old Ahafid curse.

[Exit Smerdis.]

[Re-enter Ahafid.]

Ahafid

[Sings.]

Persia's heart is beating low,
Thinking of the long ago,
When the king that wore the crown
Was a prince of great renown;
When her name without a peer
Did inspire the world with fear;
But to-night her sovereign's lust
Trails her banner in the dust.

Now my life is ebbing fast,
Dreaming of the glorious past;
Feeling all the shame and smart,
Dying of a broken heart.

[Sinks to floor.]

[Curtain.]

SCENE III

Ahasuerus

Sha-ashgaz, keeper of the concubines,
Ahasuerus drinks your health
And bids you bring immediately before
The court the serpents of the Orient!
The king would have a night of revelry.

[*The court fool, Smerdis, dances out before the court.*]

Ahasuerus (Continues)

What, Smerdis, is the office of a fool?

Smerdis

To charm these serpents of the Orient!
[*Aside*] But more to furnish brains for idiot kings.

Ahasuerus

Now tell the chief musicians every one
To string his harp with golden wire and tune
His finest Persian reed to touch the heart
With joy. To-night the emperor of the East,
The monarch of the world from Babylon
To India, would show munificence
Of entertainment never seen within
The palace walls before.

Smerdis

You do forget
That night six years ago. The palace was
A blaze of light. The air was fragrant with
The breath of spice from off the Indian seas.
Ahasuerus, flushed with flattery
And wine, was mad with passion....

Ahasuerus

[*Impetuously.*]

Smerdis, charm
These serpents, if you will, your glittering words
Are meaningless to me. Carshena, let
The Jewish Esther come in Tyrian robe,
In such a gown as never Vashti wore!

Smerdis

[*Aside.*]

His orders have not always been obeyed.

Ahasuerus

And I would have my queen adorned with gems,
That diamond cluster from beyond the Ind,
Which, sparkling in her aureole of gold, bedims
The constellation of the Southern Cross.

Smerdis

[*Aside.*]

And makes the Persian peasants mourn their loss!

Ahasuerus

I say, Meheuman, this shall be a night
In which Ahasuerus feasts his friends—
A banquet for the soul, as well as flesh.

Smerdis

[*Aside.*]

A famished soul such feasting would refresh!

Ahasuerus

For who does not delight to look upon
The rhythmic beauty of voluptuous form?

Smerdis

[*Aside.*]

Cold-blooded heart a writhing snake can warm!

Ahasuerus

Whose ear is not enthralled by luscious lute,
Whose heart is not inspired by festive song!

Smerdis

[*Aside.*]

The one bowed down by tyranny and wrong!

Ahasuerus

But why has Mordecai delayed to come?
The hated sons of Haman are no more;
That reprobate who would have slain the queen
Herself to gratify his wounded pride
Has long since festered in the rain and sun.
No enemy remains alive who dares
To touch the people of the Jew that saved
The life of Persia's king. He wears my ring;
The purple of my empire is a shield
Against the world. I do not understand
Why Mordecai is late. He should be here;
The tabor and tymbrel sound anon.

Smerdis

[*Dances and capers before the king, then speaks solemnly.*]

O king, I know why Mordecai is late,
He sits once more beside the palace gate,
In sackcloth and bemoans his fate.
He sits and dreams of hills and streams
That flow through pasture lands and fields.
He sees a child of golden hair,
As happy as the vibrant air,
And hears the notes and pulse of song
Where birds and sheep and shepherds throng.
And then he turns to banquet halls
And scenes like this in palace walls,
Where lords and queens and fools and kings,
And concubines and underlings,
Made one with wine and passion's thrall,
Throw dice with Death, nor heed the call
That comes from Persia's bleeding heart,
[*Aside*] (A fool that can not play his part).
And this explains why he is late,
The Jew beside the palace gate.

Ahasuerus

You are a jester, not a bard. Your cap
And bells, or else Death wins his throw with you.
Meheuman, call the poet of the court,

The great Ahafid. Let him celebrate
This feast in song. This rhyming fool presumes
Too much upon the patience of the king.

Smerdis

Your majesty, I did but rhyme because
Ahafid's dead.

Ahasuerus

Ahafid dead? What caused
His death?

Smerdis

[*Aside.*]

A broken heart. [*Aloud.*] He broke his harp
And died of grief. [*Aside again.*] The good gray poet could
Remember real kings.

Ahasuerus

Of grief? The fool!
Well, let the younger minstrel, Saadi sing.

Saadi

[*Sings.*]

Lift the voice and let us sing,
The monarch's on his throne;
Xerxes is the greatest king
The world has ever known.
Women, wine and happy song,
Let the revels ring,
Lift your voices loud and long,
For Xerxes is our king.

[*Much revel and dancing. The trumpet sounds.*]

Ahasuerus

Ahafid's death was only Persia's gain.

[*Meditatively.*]

Could Vashti look upon this gorgeous scene
The bitter tears would scald her faded cheeks
At thoughts of her own folly.

[*Confusion and much disturbance. Ahasuerus, surprised, cries in angry passion.*]

Ho! What means
This rude confusion? Who has dared disturb
The king in this unwonted way?

[*Enter messenger.*]

Messenger

Tidings,
O king, of riot and revolt!

Ahasuerus

Restore
The court to order. I will hear no news!
There is no news but this night's joy. What fear
Need Persia have? The world is safe;
The emperor lives! Go put the messengers to death!
This is no time to cloud the royal brow!
Bring forth the vintage from the deepest vault.
Here are a hundred irised pearls. They cost
A million sesterces. Let each man crush
A lustrous shell and drink it to the health
Of Esther, beauteous queen of all the East.
Arise! She comes! A blaze of splendor. Now
Let every instrument be sounded.
The revels shall continue till the dawn!

Zeresh

[*Rushing in with uplifted dagger and thrusting it into the heart of Esther, crying as she flourishes it before the astonished court.*]

The dawn, O king, is breaking in the east!

[*Curtain.*]

FINIS

POEMS AND SONNETS

TO
DOCTOR W. W. RAY
PHYSICIAN, SCIENTIST, POET, MUSICIAN

To Whom
Whether in Art or Nature
Truth is Beauty and Beauty Truth,
To Whose Appreciation and Enthusiasm I Owed my Intellectual
Awakening in Youth, and Whose Friendship and Love have
Increased That Obligation Immeasureably
as the Years have Passed,

I Dedicate these Poems
With the Affection of a Full Heart

COTTON NOE

"Then why not praise the tallow-dip, the dog irons and the crane,
The kettle singing on the coals, or hanging to a chain?"

THE OLD DOG IRONS

Oh, the old, old dog irons! How the picture thrills my soul,
As I stir the ashes of the past and find this living coal:
When I blow the breath of memory it flashes into flame,
That seems to me far brighter than the most undying fame.
Will you listen to the story of my early childhood days
When I read the mystic symbols in the embers and the blaze
Of the old wide-open fireplace, where the backlog, all aglow
With its shifting scenes of fancy, was a motion picture show?
I know about your natural gas, your stoves and anthracite,
Your phonograph and telephone and incandescent light;
I've heard about the comforts and the use of gasoline,
And the educative value of a Pathe photo-scene;
The future of the biplane and the wonders of the press,
And the blessings of the wireless when a ship is in distress.
I marvel at invention and its all but magic art,
But the things that make for happiness concern the human heart.
Then why not praise the tallow dip, the dog irons and the crane,
The kettle singing on the coals, or hanging to a chain?
The children gathered round the hearth to hear of early days—
The wildcat and the panther, the redman's sneaking ways;
The bravery of our fathers, the scalping knife and gun,
The courage of the women folks; I tell you, boys, 'twas fun.
We roasted sweet potatoes and we talked of Marion's men,
How they routed all the redcoats, or slew them in the fen.
We learned to love our country and we swore to tell the truth,
And do no deed of treachery and never act uncouth;
To guard the honor of our name, and shield a virtuous home,
To read the Proverbs and the Psalms and love the sacred tome.
I know our home was humble then—rag carpet on the floor—
But the stranger found a welcome there, the latch-string on the door.
The well-sweep and the woodpile and the ox team in the shed,
Dried apples hung around the walls, and pumpkins overhead—
Not sanitary, I'll admit, nor stylish-like, nor rich,
But health and comfort and content; now tell me, which is which?
Then who can blame me that I love the good old dog iron days,
When men had hearts and character that fortune couldn't faze;
The years before the slitted skirts and the Turkish cigarettes,

When women wove their linsey clothes instead of devilish nets;
When children did the chores at night, nor ever heard of gym,
Or movements such as boy scouts, yet kept in health and trim.
We spent our evenings all at home, and read and sang and played,
Or talked of work and feats of strength, or what our crops had made;
And when we mentioned quilting bees and apple-peeling time,
We had in mind our sweethearts and we sometimes made a rhyme:
'Twas then I read my future in the embers and the blaze,
And this is why I celebrate the good old dog iron ways.

THE AGE ELECTRIC

The glory of the good old days has passed from earth away,
The lumbering loom, the spinning wheel, Maud Muller raking hay;
The old rail fence, the moldboard plough, the scythe and reaping hook,
Corn shuckings, and Virginia reel, and young folks' bashful look.
Now poor old father limps behind his motorcycle son
And sees the world go whizzing by and knows his race is run.
With rheumatism in his joints and crotchets in his brain,
He finds that he can hardly catch th' accommodation train.
Two dozen bottles of the oil of Dr. Up-To-Date
Would put to flight the rheumatiz and straighten out his pate;
But fogy folks don't have the faith, nor interest in the race,
They'd rather drive a slow coach horse than go at such a pace.
Efficiency! efficiency! In business, church and school,
Where Culture in a dunce's cap sits grinning on a stool,
And wondering where the thing will end, and what the prize will be,
When Intellect, all geared and greased, is mere machinery.
Old Homer and the Iliad, the Trojan and the Greek,
The Parthenon and Phidias, not ancient, but antique.
Great Cæsar and the Gallic War and Virgil with his rhyme,
And Cicero have all gone down beneath the wheel of time.
And Dante now lies buried deep beneath the art debris,
Where Michael Angelo once wrought for immortality.
The Swan of Avon's not in school, but on the movie screen,
The Prince of Denmark can not talk but still he may be seen.
All history and literature, philosophy and truth
Would take about three evenings off of any modern youth
To master through the picture art if he the time could spare,
From vaudeville shows and joy rides and tango with the fair.
The problem is to find an hour so busy is the age,
And so important is the work and tempting is the wage.
Then what's the use of poetry or history anyhow?
Best turn your back upon the past and face the present *now*!
Get busy, and be on the job, the world will pay for skill.
It says: "Deliver me the goods, and then present your bill."
The family circle and the talk around the old hearth stone,
The sage advice, when backlogs glowed and grease lamps dimly shone,
Are mouldy pictures of the past, mere myths of long ago,

When grandsires had found out some things that children didn't know.
How many bushels can you raise upon your plot of ground?
How many blades of grass now grow where once just one was found?
Oh! Nature is the proper theme, but better Wordsworth drop,
San Jose scale and coddling moth will get your apple crop.
Ben Johnson and Will Shakespeare and Goldsmith all are dead.
Put nodules in alfalfa roots not dramas in your head.
Tomato canning's orthodox if done with due dispatch,
Don't let your daughter dream of fame, just show her how to patch.
The laws of sanitation soon will put the fly to flight,
Then stop tuberculosis next and win the hookworm fight.
If man could live a century it may be in the strife,
He'd learn to make a *living* if he didn't make a *life*!
What matter if the primrose is beside the river's brim,
A yellow primrose growing there and nothing more to him,
He's caught the trick of sustenance (but lost his taste for rhyme),
Though the oxen in the clover fields have had that all the time!

GRANDMOTHER DAYS

Ah, Grandmother Young was wrinkled and old
When she sat by the mantelpiece;
And she wore a cap with many a fold
Of ribbon and lace, as rich as gold,
And worked in many a crease:
And the billowy clouds of smoke that rolled
From her little stone pipe whenever she told
Of the quest of the Golden Fleece,
Wrought me to think that Grandmother Young
Was shriveled and gray when Homer sung
Of the gods of ancient Greece.

But all of her marvelous mythical lore
Was naught to her magical power—
Transforming a house with a puncheon floor
To a palace of wealth with a golden door
That lead to a castle tower—
An attic loft with a wonderful store
Of things that we feared, but longed to explore—
Our grandmother's ancient dower.
Oh, grandmother's charm could change but a base
Rude vessel of clay to a Haviland vase,
A weed to a royal flower.

Ah, grandmother's home was a temple of grace
And my child-heart worshipped there,
When Balm-of-Gilead around the place,
Like incense, for a mile of space,
Perfumed the glorious air;
And the song that came from the feathered race
In the boughs of the tangled interlace
Of apple and peach and pear,
Enthralled me like the magic spell
Of siren music when it fell
On old Ulysses' ear.

Last summer I passed where the palace once stood
Whose beauty my life beguiled;
It's a cabin now; and the charmed wood

Of sugar and oak, in brotherhood
Of walnut and hickory, aisled
For gathering nuts and the merry mood
That only our childhood understood,
By man has been defiled.
Oh, how can I ever cease to praise
The fairy enchantment of grandmother days
When I was a little child!

JUST TO DREAM

Just to dream when sapphire skies
Are as blue as maidens' eyes;
Just to dream when petals sow
All the earth with pink and snow;
Just to sit by youth's bright stream,
Gazing at its crystal gleam —
Listening to the wren and dove —
Hearing only songs of love —
Just to dream.

Just to dream of sabre's flash
When the lines of battle clash;
See the army put to rout —
Hear the world's triumphant shout;
Just to dream our name supreme —
Hero of a poet's theme,
First among the sons of men,
Master of the sword or pen —
Just to dream.

Just to dream when skies grow gray,
Just to dream the days away —
Living over childhood's joys,
Sorrow that no longer cloys;
Just to muse of days that seem
Like the sunlight's golden beam,
Summer nights and winter's snow.
Just to dream of long ago —
Just to dream.

AMNEMON

"Dear, the struggle has been hard and long—
The wine-press I have trodden,
Paved with flint and shard;
And many times my feet have stained
The flagstones of the street with blood.
Out yonder in the park where life's rich chalice
Sparkles with the wine of happiness and love
The world was always dull and dark to me.
Hours I have stood upon the beach
And watched the whitecaps glinting
In the sunlight and listened to the breakers
Booming on the sinuous shore,
While little children clapped their hands
And shouted out across the waters,
And gray-haired men and women shook their heads
In silence and looked toward the sunset.
But everything was always meaningless to me.
Season after season I have watched the butterflies
By millions come and go
And katydids each year have sung
The song monotonous and passed away.
Yesterday the sun arose upon another world.
Gray skies have turned to brilliant blue;
The droning hum of beetles on the breeze
Is like an orchestra of lovely music.
The air is sweet and fresh as dewdrops in convolvuli.
For two bright hours I have strolled
Among the flowering shrubbery near the seashore,
Listening to a song I had not heard for years.
And now once more that I am happy,
May I not confess it all?
I did you wrong, great wrong.
There was no stain upon my life,
No taint of blood within my veins.
I came of Pilgrim stock, vigorous and strong.
I did not understand my heart,
And knowing all the stress you placed upon heredity,

I told a falsehood, partly as a test of love,
And part for self-protection.
I have suffered much, but justly.
You said my story broke your heart,
And left me where I stood,
Pondering on the sin I had committed.
I had proved your love, but all too late.
Your talent meant a brilliant future,
And I knew your great ambition.
For years I scanned the periodicals
Where names of most renown in literature are found,
Expecting always to see my lover's there,
But always doomed to disappointment.
And yet I now rejoice
That you have not achieved great fame,
For otherwise I could not write this letter.
Perhaps 'twere best that I should never send it;
If so, it will not find its way to you.
It may be that you think me dead,
Or worse—I may have been forgotten.
This is April twenty-first;
The hillsides now are pink with peach and apple bloom.
I will arrive in Salt Lake City, May the third,
And be at Hotel Utah.
If your heart, through all these years,
Like mine, has hungered, you will be there too.
Geraldine."

Alfred Milner read this letter
While great drops of perspiration
Stood upon his brow and trembling hand.
For seven winters he had tried
To bury in oblivion a face and form
That always with the dogwood blossoms
Came again, and each time seemed more fair.
He had tried for fame and failed.
But now his book that bore a pen name only
Was selling daily by the thousands
And fame and fortune, latter-day twin saints,
Were building him a shrine.
But did she know of his success,
And was her conduct
Years before base cowardice?
Had she only told the cruel tale
Because she knew his theory of insane blood,
And hid her lack of faith
By taking refuge in his prejudice?

Or was her story true?
If true or false, why had she kept it back
Until she knew red passion
Was a-riot in his heart?
He tore the letter into strips
And blew them fiercely through the air.
He had suffered much himself,
But she was not concerned.
What if this letter had been sent
To open healing wounds,
To win some wager with another man
To whom she boasted of her power?
He would not go!

The air was growing foul and stuffy
In his suite of rooms,
And Alfred threw the window open.
The subway in the distance
Rumbled like a gathering storm;
The palisades across the Hudson
Now were darkling in the falling shadows.

April thirtieth at noon.
The Rocky Mountains looked like towers
On the Chinese Wall a hundred miles away.
Would he make connection at Pueblo?
The gray monotony of grass and cacti
Had begun to wear upon his nerves.
He longed to see the Royal Gorge—
The steep and jagged heights of hills.
They spoke of giant strength
He needed for the coming struggle.
It might be that the air
From off eternal snows
Would cool the fever in his brain.

"May second, and yonder lies the Great Salt Lake,
Or else a mirage on the desert's rim."

Alfred put his pen upon the register
Of Hotel Utah,
And read the list of names above.
She was there, "Geraldine Mahaffy."
Finally he scrawled a signature,
But wrote his *nom de plume*.
The clerk thrust out his hand and beamed.
Two porters swooped upon his grips,
And soon the lobby hummed.
But Alfred Milner sat alone within his room

Battling with emotions he could neither
Overcome nor understand.
He did not know the stir his name upon the register
Had made below, or knew what name he wrote.
At last: "Geraldine Mahaffy:
This is May the third and I am here."
Thoughtfully he creased the sheet
And rang: "Room ten, and answer, please."

The smell of brine was heavy on the air
That blew across the lake.
The mountains to the north were white with snow above
And dogwood petals on the southern slopes.
But winter was forgotten in the plains,
For rivulets imprisoned long in cataracts
Were leaping over waterfalls
And shouting like a red bird,
In an April cedar tree.

Milner drew a long deep breath of spring
And walked into the parlor.
"Alfred!"
"Geraldine!"

"Last night I dreamed of Cornell days,
And saw the redbuds blooming in the hills
Behind the cliffs of Ithaca!"

"The ice in Cascadilla Creek is gone.
All night I heard the roaring of the falls!"

"The call of flickers sounded through the canyons
Of Old Buttermilk, and peckerwoods were beating
Reveilles before the sun was up!"

"Two blue birds built a mansion
In a dead oak trunk
And called the world to witness!"

"Alfred!"
"Geraldine!"

"The train for California leaves at nine!"

Some hours out from Great Salt Lake,
The sand dunes stretching southward
O'er a waste of shrubbery and alkali
Were shimmering in the sunshine
Like copper kettles on a field of bronze.

"Dear Alfred, can you still recall
Those afternoons upon the cliffs above Cayuga Lake?
The little city, Ithaca,

Was like a jewel on the breast of Nature.
The lake a band of silver, stretching northward.
A hundred waterfalls were visible
From where we used to sit.
We often thought the lime-washed houses
Far to west, resembled whited decks
Upon a sea of emerald;
And wondered if our own good ship
Would one day cast its anchor in the harbor.
Over to the right the Cornell towers,
Like mediæval castles beetling o'er the precipice,
Were keeping silent watch above it all.
The memory of those blessed days alone
Has kept my heart alive."

"But Geraldine, our vessel richly laden
Has at last come in
Nor ever will put out to sea again.
Happy as those moments were,
Forget the past, so fraught with bitterness to me."

The desert now a hundred miles behind
Was fading like a crescent sea beach
In the setting sun.
Slowly like a giant serpent
The Sunset Limited climbed the great Sierras
And started down the western slope at dawn.
The valley of the Sacramento
Never bloomed so beautiful before.
The blue Pacific through the haze
Was like a canvas sea.
Peace permeated all the earth.
The sun at last was resting on the ocean's rim.
The turquoise waters turned to liquid gold.

"Life, O my beloved, is like eternal seas—
Emerald in the morning, changing into opal,
Amethyst and pearl, but ruby red at last.
Behold the Golden Gate!
The seas beyond are all like that!"

Morning in the Sacramento!
Petals, dew and fragrance—indescribable!
Plumage, song and sunshine,
And over all a California sky!

"O Alfred, could it only be like this forever!
Back yonder in New York,
The world is built of brick and mortar,

And men forget the handiwork of God.
How can a poet hope to win a name
Where men are mad for gold?"

"A name! Why Geraldine! I had forgot
To tell the story of my fame.
The ecstacy of these three days
Had blotted all earthly fortune from my memory.
I am Ralph Nixon, author of the *Topaz Mystery*."

"Ralph Nixon! You! Then who am I?"
A heavy tide of blood swept over
All the tracery of the bitter past,
And in a moment more
She lay unconscious on a bed of thorny cactus.

The *City Argentina* blew a long loud blast
And anchored in the bay.
The woman opened wondering eyes
And looked at Milner.
"Why do you call me Geraldine?
My Christian name's Amnemon.
We never met before.
I am Major Erskine's wife.
We live in Pasadena.
I do not know your name or face,
Nor how I came to be with you.
I never saw this place before,
But those are California hills
And yonder is the great Pacific.
The mystery of who you are,
And where I am, I can not solve.
I only know I wish to see my home and child;
Little Alfred never has been left alone,
And may be calling for his mother now.
You seem to be a gentleman.
Please show me to the nearest train
That goes to Pasadena."

Half in fright and half in rage
Milner looked at Geraldine and tried to speak.
The mountains reeled and pitched into the sea.
A clevage in the brain! But whose?
This was insanity, but whether his
Or hers he was unable to decide.
The memory of the Cornell days came back—
The cliffs above the lake, the emerald farms,
The gorges and the waterfalls,
And finally the wild, weird light

That played in iridescent eyes
That last day on the hills—
The story of the tainted blood and what it meant
For future generations.
Milner saw an eagle soaring high above the park
And then he heard a scream
As though a ball had pierced its heart.
The bird careened and dropped a hundred feet,
Then spreading broad its wings again,
Shot upward to the heights.

The train for Pasadena speeded onward
Toward its destination.
A poet sat within his room
That opened on the Golden Gate
And as the sun dropped into the wave,
He wrote a Requiem to Hope,
That filled the earth with fame.

A ROMANCE OF THE CUMBERLAND

Early in the day they passed the pinnacle,
And now the shadow of each human form
Was lengthening backwards like Lombardy poplars
Fallen toward the east.
For days the fairest maiden of the caravan
Had fevered—whether from malaria and fatigue,
Or more because of one whom they had left behind,
Beyond the wooded mountains,
Neither sire nor matron could agree.
But Martha Waters, as they laid her stretcher down
And prepared the camp for coming night,
Declared unless they rested here for days to come,
Her bones must bleach beside the trail
That led into the Dark and Bloody Ground.

And so they waited for the fever to abate,
But when they thought her strong enough,
A score of hardy pioneers trudged down
The slope and launched canoes and dug-outs
And a flatboat in the turgid waters
Of the Cumberland, for heavy rains had fallen
And all the mountain streams were swollen
In these early days of June.
But the air was sweet with the odor
Of wild honeysuckle and the ivy
With its starry clusters fringed
The milky way of elder bloom
That filled each sheltered cove
Like constellations on a summer night.
But now the rains had ceased, the air
Was fresh and bracing, and each glorious day
Out-rivaled all the rest in beauty.
Lying on her pallet on the flatboat,
The maiden breathed the fragrant atmosphere,
And drank refreshing whiffs of air
That drove the fever from her blood
And wakened dreams of conquest
In the wilderness toward which

Her life was drifting rapidly.
But how could she find heart for conquest?
Why seek this new land anyway, where only
And forever to card the wool and spin the flax
Would be the woman's portion?
Would ever in the forest or beyond it
In the rolling bluegrass,
Return the vision that was hers,
When only a few brief months ago
She watched the sea gulls battling with the storm
Above the waves of Chesapeake Bay?
Oh, how that day was filled with meaning
For her now! For as the birds disported
With the whirlpools of the air,
A lover's magic words were whispered in her ear,
How that storm and stress of life to those that love
Are little more than winds to swallows of the sea.
But now, if hardship meant so little,
Why had he remained behind, when she
Was forced to go upon the long and weary journey?
Ah! Could it be he cared no longer for her love?
His arm was strong. Then was his heart
Not brave enough to conquer this new world,
Where savage lurked and wild beast made
The darkness dreaded by the most courageous soul?

For days the fleet had drifted down the river,
But now her boat was anchored to a tree
That grew upon an island in the Cumberland,
And every man and woman but the convalescent
Had gone ashore to stalk a deer or gather berries
That everywhere were found along the river bank.
But Martha Waters lay upon her bed and pondered—
Dreaming day dreams, as she watched
A golden oriole who fed her young
In boughs that overhung the water,
And a vague unhappiness arose
Within her heart, until she tossed
Again in fever on her couch.
She could hear the roaring falls
A mile below, but she thought the sounding
Cataract the sickness booming in her ears again.
When she looked to eastward where the mountain
Rose a thousand feet, she saw a crown of wealth
Upon its crest of which no pioneer yet had dreamed.
Long she lay and marveled at its beauty,
Wondering how many ages would elapse before

The god of Mammon would transport its treasures
To his marts beside the sea.
Feverish she mused and pondered until at last she slept.
And then upon the little island,
A city rose as from the ocean wave—
A city of a thousand streets, and every house
Was made from trees that grew upon the mountain.
Many were the palaces of wealth and beauty,
But those who dwelt therein she did not recognize.
Strange were their faces and their manners haughty,
And while they lived in luxury and ease,
Others toiled at mill and furnace. Oh! The awful din
Of sledge and hammer, beating in her ears.
She woke. A storm seemed just about to burst in fury,
So loud and terrible was the roaring!
But the sky was clear. It is the booming
Of the falls, for her boat has broke its moorings,
And now is rapidly drifting toward the cataract,
But four hundred yards away!

She leaped upon her feet and screamed for help.
It was impossible for her to swim ashore,
And her fever-wasted frame could find no strength
With which to steer the boat.
Again she saw the crown of wealth
Upon the mountain top, untouched by human hands.
But the island city now had faded from her vision,
The mountain lowered and the world grew dark.
Onward the boat shot faster toward the roaring falls.
But look! A race is on! A birch canoe,
Driven by as swift a hand as ever gripped
An oar, is leaping o'er the waves in mad pursuit.
With every stroke the Indian bark is gaining twenty feet.
Will it reach the flatboat soon enough to save the girl?
But who is he that rides the fleet canoe?
No red man ever had an arm like that,
For already he has reached the speeding raft,
And with gigantic strength he steers it toward the shore.
But no! The current is too swift!
A moment more and all will be engulfed within
The swirling flood. It is too late! Too late?
But love is swifter than the angry tide,
For like a mighty porpoise, wallowing in the wave,
The valiant hero leaps into the stream,
And holding Martha Waters in his strong right arm
High above the water, reaches shore
A hundred feet above the deadly precipice.

The air was growing chilly even on this summer night,
And the emigrants had gathered round a crackling fire,
Discoursing of the past, and listening to a modest tale of love.
Simply and unfaltering James Hunt related
How his heart had hungered back beside the old Potomac,
Till he found he could no longer brook the passion
That grew stronger as the days of summer lengthened.
At last he started, and following every night
The blazing dogstar, and resting through the day till evening,
In just three weeks he reached the river
Where he found the birch canoe that rode
The seething waters like a greyhound of the ocean.
Then the maiden told her vision of the island city,
How its palaces and mansions, rich as gold and beautiful as crystal,
Were constructed by her people, toiling hundreds,
Sore and weary, of times cold and hungry.
She had seen them fell the forests,
Hew and mill and dress the lumber,
Till the soil and reap the harvests, gathering into others' garners.
Stalwart were these men and women, pure of heart
And strong of muscle, fitted for the tasks before them.
She had seen her brothers laboring at the forge and sounding anvil;
Sisters toiling at the wheel and distaff, heard them at the loom
While flying shuttle threaded warp with web of beauty;
Watched them till they fell asleep with weariness,
While the sons of leisure feasted.
Thus the maiden told her story, saying:
"Shall we undertake the journey? Plows are waiting
In the furrows back in Maryland, my people,
Back beyond the rugged mountain. There are harvests
Yet ungarnered, waiting for scythe and sickle.
Calculate the cost, and weigh it, for my vision is prophetic.
For my part, I choose this lover, for my guide and valiant leader.
He shall point the way forever,
Though he take the road that's darkest."

Then James Hunt, the hero lover,
Who had never quailed at danger,
Trembling for his happy passion,
Rose and pointed toward the westward,
Toward the Pleiades descending,
Deep behind the gloomy forest.
"Let us face toward dark Kentucky, fell its forests,
Build its roads and bridge its rivers,
Give our children to the nation.
What though others reap our harvests,
Hoard the wealth we have created?

Ours shall be the nobler portion.
Blessed is the one that suffers,
If he spends himself for others.
Should the toiling millions falter,
Though they work for others' comfort,
Building homes they can not enter?
Christ was born within a manger,
May we not produce a leader,
Who shall save our nation's honor?
At to-morrow morning's dawning,
Ere the sunrise gild the treetops,
Let us take the darkling pathway."

Still the Pleiades are circling,
Still the dogstar glows in heaven,
But the oak and pine and poplar
All have gone from off the mountain—
Passed into the marts of Mammon,
By the hands of toil and labor.
Silent are the loom and distaff,
In the cabin and the cottage,
And the songs of scythe and sickle
Gathering in the golden harvests.
But the pain of drudgery lingers,
And the heart still longs and hungers
For the fruitage it shall gather,
Yet beyond the wooded westward.

MORNING GLORIES.

A roguish laugh, a rustling vine,
I turn my eager eye;
Big drops of dew in bells of blue
And red convolvuli.

But nothing more; I hold my breath
And strain my eager eye;
A yellow crown, two eyes of brown,
And pink convolvuli!

The golden curls, the elfish laugh,
Rose cheeks and glittering eye
Are glories, too, like bells of blue
And red convolvuli.

CHRISTMASTIDE

Evergreen and tinsel'd toys,
Drums and dolls, and bursting joys—
Blessed little girls and boys!

Holly, bells, and mistletoe,
Tinkling sledges, here we go—
Youth and maiden o'er the snow.

Chilling winds and leaden days,
Vesper songs and hymns of praise
Silver hair and dying blaze!

Christmas morn and yuletide eve,
Dear Lord, help us to believe—
Naught but blessings we receive.

KINSHIP

Oh, little children, ye who watch the trains go by,
With yearning faces pressed against the window panes,
You do not know the reason why
Your lingering image dims my eye
Though I have passed beyond the hills into the rolling plains.

Dear little children, I once watched the trains go by,
And hungered, much as when I feel the silent stars;
And then I saw the cold gray skies,
And felt the warm tears in my eyes,
When far beyond the distant hills I heard the rumbling cars.

PRECOCITY

"Oh, grandfather, what are the stars?
Stones on the hand of God?
I heard you call that red one Mars
And those three Aaron's rod;
And these are great Orion's band!"
"My child, you are too young to understand!"

"Oh, grandfather, what are the winds
That sough and moan and sigh?
Does God grow angry for men's sins
He lifts the waves so high?
And blows his breath o'er sea and land?"
"My boy, you are too young to understand!"

"Oh, grandfather, what are the clouds
In yonder sunset sky?
They look to me like winding shrouds
For men about to die!
Dear grandfather, your trembling hand!"
"My son, you are too young to understand!"

THE SECRET

Old Santa Claus came with his pack
On his back
Right down the chimney flue;
His long flowing beard was ghostlike and weird
But his cheeks had a ruddy hue;
And his jacket was as red as a woodpecker's head
But his breeches, I think, were blue.

I heard a soft step like a hoof
On the roof,
And I closed my outside eye;
Then played-like I slept, but the other eye kept
A watch on the jolly old guy;
And I caught him in the act with his bundles all unpacked,
But I'm not going to tell, not I.

When Santa comes again this year
With his deer
And a sled full of toys for me,
I don't mean to keep either eye from its sleep
While he climbs my Christmas tree;
For I don't think it's right to the happy old wight
To spy on his mystery.

A RHYMELESS SONNET

Sardonic *Death*, clothed in a scarlet shroud,
Salutes his minions on the crumbling thrones
Of Tyranny, and with malicious leer,
He points a fleshless finger toward the fields
Of Belgium: "No harvest since the days
Of Bonaparte and Waterloo hath filled
My flagons with a wine of such a taste;
Your crowns ye hold by rights divine indeed!"

But *One* has entered in at lowly doors
And sits by every hearthstone where they will:
"My *Word* enthron-ed in Democracy
Has twined the holly round Columbia's brow —
A crown of 'Peace on earth, good will to men.'
I am the *Resurrection* and the *Life!*"

AMBITION

I covet not the warrior's flashing steel
That drives the dreaded foe to headlong flight;
I envy not the czar his ruthless might
That grinds a state beneath an iron heel;
I do not ask that I may ever feel
The thrill that follows fame's uncertain light;
And in the game of life I do not quite
Expect always to hold a winning deal.

Grant me the power to help my fellow man
To bear some ill that he may not deserve;
Give me the heart that I may never swerve,
In scorn of Death, to do what good I can;
But most of all let me but light the fires
Upon the altar of the *youth's* desires.

OPPORTUNITY

I often met her in the days of youth
Along the highway where the world goes by;
And sometimes when I caught her wistful eye
I wondered that it seemed so filled with ruth.
She was a modest maiden, plain, in truth,
And unattractive, and I thought, "Now why
Should one seek her companionship; not I—
At least, until I've had my fling, forsooth!"

And so I passed her by and had my day,
And met a thousand whom I thought more fair
In tinsel gowns beneath electric glare—
A thousand, but they went their primrose way.
Now she's a queen, and boasts a score of sons—
Her consort he who shunned my charming ones!

HOLIDAY THOUGHTS

The night was like some monster omen ill,
Whose shrieking froze the marrow of my bones;
But day dawned calm, though white as polar zones,
The bluebird shouting "Spring!" from every hill.
The world lay parching in the noonday grill,
And blades of corn were twisting into cones;
But night brought rain, and now, like golden thrones,
The fruited shocks deride October's chill.

Dear Lord, I would that we might live by faith,
However cold and dark the day may seem,
And trust that every cloud is just a wraith,
And every shadow but a fading dream.
Oh, grant our eyes may see the beacon lights
That blaze forever on the peaks and heights!

THE OLD YEAR AND THE NEW

Good-bye, Old Year; our journey has been brief;
I'm sorry now to leave thee dying here,
For thou hast borne my burdens with good cheer,
And never murmured, but assuaged my grief.
When buds of promise never came to leaf;
When broken resolutions, doubt, and fear
Did mock at my defeat, O good Gray Year,
Thy reassuring smile restored belief.

Good-bye—farewell! I trust thy dear young child,
Who greets me at the gateway of the dawn,
Will deal as gently with me and my friends,
And lead our footsteps through the springtime mild,
O'er summer's lawn, down autumn's slopes, and on
To where the path of chill December ends.

FELLOW TRAVELERS

Old comrade, must we separate to-day?
Sometimes my feet have faltered, sore and tired,
And sometimes in the sloughs and quicksands mired,
But it has always helped to hear you say,
"The road is fine a little further on."
Your optimism and your hearty cheer
Have made the journey pleasant, good Old Year,
And I, in truth, regret to see you gone.

Young New Year whom you leave me as a guide,
In doubt, would have me pledge a lot of things
Before we start, and make some offerings
To gods whose love, I fear, will not abide.
And yet I like my new companion's face.
Old Year, lend him your wisdom and your grace.

JAMES WHITCOMB RILEY

Beloved Poet, thou hast taught our heart
A sympathy it hardly knew before—
A yearning kinship and a spirit lore
Of humble folk, a love transcending art!
The pulse of brotherhood throbs in thy song.
No mystic, blindly groping on the shore
Of dark uncertainty; unlike Tagore,
Thy faith is pure and definite and strong.

Consumpted Jim and thriftless Coon-dog Wess,
The Girly Girl with eyes of limpid blue,
The Raggedy Man that Orphant Annie knew;
The Little Cripple, glad, though motherless;
Poor hare-lip Joney and the Wandering Jew—
All these thy pen doth glorify and bless!

CALE YOUNG RICE

He loves the boom of breakers on the shore,
And winds that lash the billows into foam;
He loves the placid seas beneath the dome
Of blue infinitudes—not less, but more;
He loves to brood upon the mystic lore
Of silent stars above the silent seas,
And feel the passion of infinities
Beyond, where only Faith would dare explore.

Thus groping after God has helped him find
Divinity in man (where only sin
And brutal lusts have seemed to hedge him in),
And taught his heart that Fate is never blind.
That somehow, somewhere, now beyond our ken,
One day we'll understand the wrongs of men.

PILATE'S MONOLOGUE

[*This monologue of Pilate to Herod takes place a few days after the resurrection at the home of Pontius Pilate. Pilate and Herod are standing on the east porch of the Governor's mansion in Jerusalem, looking toward the Mount of Olives. The time is just at sunset.*]

Oh! Herod, couldst thou find no fault in Him—
The Man of Galilee? Clearly He
Belonged within thy jurisdiction. Didst
Thou fear to do thy duty? Still I blame
Thee not—the mob was clamorous for blood!
I questioned Him, but like a lamb before
His shearers He was dumb and answered me
No word. Was not His silence proof of guilt?
But even then I offered to release
Him, till the rabble shouted, "Crucify
This Man: set free Barabbas, if thou wilt,
But we demand the life of Jesus whom
They call the *Christ*." Oh! dost thou think His blood
Can be upon my head? I washed my hands
Before the multitude and told them I
Was innocent of any crime toward Him.
I scourged Him, it is true, but that was all.
They stripped Him and bedecked Him with a robe
Of scarlet cloth, and placed a crown of thorns
Upon His head, and then they mocked and jeered
And spat upon Him, hailing Him as *King*!
I can not think that this was right, but still
They say He blasphemed and deserved to die.
But what Is blasphemy?
Oh, Herod, I
Can never rid my dreams of Jesus' look.
He turned His eyes upon me as I dipped
My fingers in the bowl—a glance that seemed
More fraught with love and pity than with hate.
He blessed the people as He hung upon
The cross in agony of pain, and prayed
His God to pardon them because they knew
Not what they did. Thou canst not, Herod, think
This Nazarene was more than man? It can't

Be possible that He whom Pilate scourged
Was *Christ* indeed! But could a *man* forgive
His murderers? They say the tomb is burst
And that His body is no longer there!
I might endure His curse. My pen has stabbed
To death a thousand men and never felt
Compunction for the deed, because I knew
They hated me. But now the voice that haunts
My sleep asks only blessings on my head.
They say He wept for men because of sin,
And yet no guile was found in Him. If I
Could close my eyes and see that face no more
I might find peace again.
Three nights I have
Not slept. I hear that Judas hanged himself!
And now no guard that watched before
The sepulchre can anywhere be found.
Had I but set the Galilean free!
But did he not insult my majesty?
He must have known I ruled in Cæsar's stead.
What if my wife was troubled in a dream
And suffered many things on His account?
A Roman governor must be a man!
They say the temple's veil was rent in twain—
The sky was darkened and the sun was hid.
He said I had no power to crucify
Except that it be given from above.
He did not know the strength of Pilate's arm!
'Tis said He cried, "My God, my God, why hast
Thou now forsaken me?" The earth did quake,
The tombs were cracked, and then the shrouded dead
Stalked ghost-like through the fields and open streets!
Look! Look! What is yon robe of shining white?
Behold the Man—the Man of Galilee!
With outstretched arms He stands on Olivet,
The shadows purpling o'er Gethsemane.
I hear Him cry in agony of soul,
"How often would I, O Jerusalem,
Have gathered unto Me thy children as
A hen her brood beneath her wing, but ye
Would not come." Herod, canst thou hear His voice?
It is impossible! It can not be!
He must not know that I am Pilate! Still
He calls my name! I can not, dare not go!
What would the people think? I will
Be free. There is no blood upon my hands.

See, I wash them clean and am myself
Again. Oh! Now the spell is gone. Though not
The king, I am governor of the Jews!

THE VIRILE SPIRIT

[*Written after reading a letter in which the writer said: "I covet for our country a great war—one that will stir our virile spirits and send forth our youth to fight and die for our country."*]

What is courage? To face the bursting shell
When rhythmic sheets of fire discover gulfs
Of death, yet rather steel than daunt the heart;
When comrades fall beneath the knapsack's weight,
Foot froze and bleeding on the icy road,
To hear the blasts from towering snow-crowned Alps
Sing only martial airs that stir the blood!
It is a noble thing to die in war—
To sacrifice the breath of life; to feel
The pain of hunger and of cold, yet flinch
Not that one's country may be great or free.
Many a generation yet unborn
Will bless the name of Valley Forge, and hold
In reverence the field of Gettysburg.
But war is not the only thing that tries
The bravest soul. To live does sometimes take
More courage than to close with death; and oft
The coward shrinks from living when the brave
Man scorns to die. We need no bugle note
To rouse our manhood's strength. The call to men
Is clear and strong. It is not to repel
The Hun, the Teuton, or the Slav, nor yet
To drive the Yellow Peril from the seas.
We must send forth our men to live, not die—
We need to save, not kill our fellow man,
To smite the Minotaur of Sin, and stop
The tribute greater now than all the tolls
Of war. The beast in man is ravenous
And must be slain. He feeds upon the fruits
Of toil, and blights the home with poverty;
He drags the innocent to dens of shame
To satisfy his brute carnality.
No fiery dragon in the days of myth
Laid waste a land or blasted life with breath

More foul or appetite insatiate.
This is the enemy that we must fight.
No dreadnaughts now afloat, no submarines,
No legions that may ever bivouac on
Our shores, no Zeppelins disgorging fire
Portend the dire disasters wrought upon
Our nation's strength by Avarice and Lust.
The sword of Theseus is too dull a blade,
The arm of Beowulf not strong enough
To battle with Cupidity and Sin.
We need the breastplate of a righteous life,
Our loins must be girt about with truth,
The heart protected by the shield of faith,
And in the right hand there must ever be
The spirit's sword, which is the Word of God!
And even clothed and weaponed thus it takes
A heart as fearless as the dauntless Dane's
To strike the Mammon of Unrighteousness—
To grapple with this Grendel that invades
The mead-halls still and ravishes our youth.

BLUEBIRD.

Bluebird in the cedar bush—
Fresh and clean as the evergreen,
Through a rift of leaves,
Or my eye deceives.
But silent! Hush!
He calls, he calls!
The first spring note
From a feathered throat
My heart enthralls;
And my pulses leap
As a child from sleep
On Christmas morn, at the blast of horn,
To meet, to greet,
The choral sweet
From bluebird in the cedar bush:
At last, at last
The snow and sleet
Of winter's blast
Have passed, have passed,
And spring is here, good cheer, good cheer!
The call comes ringing in to me
From Bluebird in the cedar tree.

AN AUTUMN MINOR

Russet and amber and gold,
Crimson and yellow and green,
And far away the blue and gray,
A twinkling silver sheen.

Violet, scarlet and red,
Purple and dark maroon,
And over it all the music of fall—
A weird prismatic tune.

An opera serious and grand,
An orchestra mystic and sad—
A symphony alone of color and tone
To drive a mortal mad.

SLABS AND OBELISK

Hollyhocks were blooming in the backyard near the barn,
Proud as rhododendrons by a regal mountain tarn,
Purple, white and yellow, blue and velvet red—
Humble little cottage, but a royal flower bed.
Pink and crimson roses and carnations took your breath—
Dark-eyed little pansies looking like the Head of Death;
Golden-rayed sunflowers, lifting discs of hazel brown,
Filled the heart with wonder and the garden with renown.

Little Harold, born a poet, watched the petals blow,
Read the mystic cryptographs his elders didn't know;
Heard the music in the wind like sirens on the shore,
Far beyond the sunset in the land Forevermore.
Oft the village sages saw him lying in the shade,
Gazing where the sun and vapor wrought a strange brocade—
Tapestries of gold and silver on a field of blue,
Heard him murmur softly riddles no one ever knew.

All the people pitied Harold, thinking of the end
In the cold, unfeeling world he couldn't comprehend—
Seeing nothing else but lilies, living in a trance,
In an age of facts and figures, dreaming wild romance.
But the sages now are sleeping on the little hill,
Modest slabs are keeping watch with rue and daffodil.
Harold has an obelisk that towers toward the sky,
Hollyhocks upon his mound to bless and glorify.

ON BROADWAY

Even as to-night on Broadway
Long ago I wandered down
The Great White Way of childhood,
Mystified, enchanted, as I watched
The million butterflies
That tilted through the air in rhythmic flight,
And pulsed above the petaled sweets,
And sipped the nectar of the purple thistle bloom,
Until at last they staggered down the dusty Road to Death.

POSTSCRIPT

AN EMBER ETCHING

An old man sat before his great log fire
And gazed dreamily into the dying blaze.
His eyes were red as though with weeping.
The long, thin locks of hair
Were spotless as the snow
Silently mantling the earth
That last sad night of the dying year.
Four days and nights
He had sat beside the bed
Of his life-companion.
But now the watchers by the bier
In the adjoining room,
Were dozing in their chairs.
The cold night
Had driven the mice from their hiding,
And the loud tick of the clock
No longer frightened them
As they scampered over the hearth.

The man was breathing heavily,
Although his eyes were open,
And his stare fixed upon the fire:
Down by a gnarled oak near the spring
Two children played.
Rebecca had dipped a dock leaf
In the water,
And now whisked it in the sunlight.
Against the trunk of the tree
There was a playhouse made of broken boughs.
The girl's dolls were lying on the green moss bed,
And a little cracked slate lay upon the ground.
An almost illegible scrawl was written on the slate.
Two childish hands had traced their names:
"Rupert—Rebecca."
And the words were linked together by lines
That looked like twisted ropes.
The boy and girl sat down before the playhouse,
And crossed their hands in imitation

Of the lines that bound their names together.
And then they smiled
And looked upon the dolls
Asleep in the fresh June morning.

A chunk broke and fell in the ashes.
The blaze died into a glow of coals.
In the gray beyond the dog irons
The old man saw two figures
Sitting before an awning:
Two golden haired children
Slept in a little bed.
The man and woman who sat beside the shelter
Were old and bent,
Their faces thin and white.
They clasped their hands
And looked into each other's face.
And then they turned and looked
Upon the children.
A coal dropped into the picture,
And the fitful fire died
Into deepening shadows.

Next day the pall-bearers
Bore two bodies away
And lowered a single coffin
Into a grave
Beneath the snow-laden cedar.

A TRAGEDY IN BIRDLAND

A little maiden blue-jay,
Fresh from her April morning bath,
Sat on the limb of a weeping willow,
Preening her shining feathers
And dreaming of a song
To which she had listened
On the afternoon of the preceding day.
A wild joy was in her heart
And yet it took all the sunshine and song
From a hundred other throats
To withstand the gloom
That seemed hovering just above her.
She was conscious of the threatening cloud,
But her heart beat furiously
And hope thrilled her bird-being
With an unwonted light.
And yet she knew,
When she dared to think at all,
That it was a hopeless hope
That flooded her soul with love—
A hope that must ere long
Change to a black despair.
She lifted her crested head
And looked toward the old beech tree
Where her blue-jay lover now sat
In melancholy gloom.
Why not raise her voice
And gladden his heart?
He had been true and faithful
For many weeks,
And his suit would long since
Have won another's love.
Why had she thrilled
At the alien voice of another throat?
She had been a foolish maiden
To have entertained so wild a thought.

But hark! Again the song!
On the topmost spire
Of yonder Gothic poplar
Sits a cardinal fop,
In a coat of matchless red,
And a beak of shining ivory.
He lifts his sumach plume
Into the glinting sunlight
And sends a Cupid shaft
From his beaded eye
Into the trembling breast
Of little maiden blue-jay.
Poor little mademoiselle!
Once more the notes
Come whistling and glittering
Like a shower of pearls
Through the sunshine:
"Oh! my true love is a little blue-jay—
Mademoiselle, my bird gazelle,
My little gazelle, and I love her well.
Fresh and sweet from her morning spray
She sits on the willow and her crest is gay—
Mademoiselle, my little gazelle I love so well."

Down from his commanding height
Flashed the cardinal flame
And perched on another limb
Of the weeping willow.
And then he strutted and pranced
And capered and danced
And shot his fiery glances
Toward the modest little maiden
Whose heart was now fluttering
Beyond all control. Master blue-jay
Over on the beech bough
Saw the terrible tragedy
That would follow in the wake of betrayal
And was desperate to save this Psyche
To whom he had often poured out his soul
In amorous vows,
Swearing by all the gods in birdland
That there was none other beside her.
But like many another lover
Of larger experience and better advantage,
He forgot that the very way
To lose his loved one
Was to berate his rival,

And lifting his reed
To the upper register of a clarinet,
He almost screamed:

"He's a liar, he is, by the god of all birds,
A master of villainous art—
A hypocrite, a varlet, believe not his words,
This dandy, this fop, deceiver, betrayer,
A coward, seducer, a murderous slayer—
He'll crush thy innocent heart."

Poor little maiden blue-jay
Heard his screams of anger and despair
But heeded not the warning.
She only fluttered over
To where the cardinal sat
And threw herself under his protecting arm,
Declaring her perfect faith
In his undying love.

The red prince lifted
His burning plume triumphantly
Into the sunlight,
And shot a contemptuous glance
Toward the old beech tree.
Master Blue-Jay unable
Longer to control himself,
Darted like a lance of blue steel
At the red coat.
But the high churchman was a skilled fencer,
And stepped aside just in time
To send his antagonist
With terrible momentum
Into the thorn tree
Beyond the willow,
Where a moment later he writhed and fluttered,
Pinioned through his body
By a sword-like thorn
That projected from the trunk of the spiny tree.
It was a sight to touch the heart
Of the most abandoned denizen of birdland.
But Mademoiselle Blue-Jay,
Who would ordinarily have wept
At so sad a fate of one of her kind,
Was just now too happy
In the love of her wooer
To notice another;
And unmindful of the ebbing life-blood

That was fast turning her unfortunate lover's coat
Of bright and shining blue
To one of dark and dull maroon,
She nestled close
To the false-hearted ecclesiastic
And sighed the lovelorn sigh
That has come from the maiden heart
Since the foundation of the world.

The low cedar
In which Madam Blue-Jay-Cardinal now sat
On such a nest of eggs
As no blue-jay had ever brooded over before,
Wondering, fearing, doubting, longing—
Was only a rod or so from the spiny thorn
Where the dried body of the fated lover
Still hung.
But where now was the supercilious fop
Whose seductive vows of love
Had won the little maiden's confidence
And robbed her true and faithful lover
Of that incense that belonged of right
Only to him?
For more than a week
She had not seen him.
Surely he would return on the morrow,
For he must remember
That soon the little brood
Would need his protecting love.
Yes, he would return again
To praise her slender form and shining crest
And call her once more his little gazelle.

But the cardinal came not.
The brood had hatched,
And the little birds were covered now
With tiny feathers.
Strange sight!
All the blue-jays in the woods around
Had gathered to witness
What no mortal bird had ever seen before—
Little birdling blue-jays
With crimson stains on wings and breasts!
And the poor little mother,
Madam Blue-Jay-Cardinal,
No longer mademoiselle, the bird gazelle,
But an outcast and disgraced mother

Of a mongrel offspring,
Left alone in this hour of shame,
Remembered now the words of him
Who had warned against this sad hour.

But the memory brought her only bitter grief,
And she watched her brood in broken-hearted sorrow,
As they looked with wondering eyes
At the strange panorama in birdland.
And all the blue-jays sat in silent condemnation
Of the unpardonable sin.
There was no mercy
To be found in all the land of birds
For either the forsaken mother
Or her little brood.
The deserted wife and widowed mother blue-jay
Suddenly threw her wings
Over the astonished little children,
As though to wipe the stain of sin
From their innocent lives,
And as she did so,
The crested cardinal
With a fresh crimson bride flashed by,
And perched upon the old beech limb.
And there he sat
In undisturbed and cynical silence,
While all the court
Of high crimes and misdemeanors
Praised his sacerdotal coat and shining mitre.
The mother felt the birdlings stir beneath her wing,
And their scarlet stain suffuse her being.
She looked toward the thorn tree
But no word was spoken.
A wise old owl that moped and moaned
On the limb of a sycamore tree
That overhung the little stream
Suddenly lifted his voice and cried:

"Let him who is without stain of sin,
Lift the first note of song
Against the little blue-jay."

But all the woods were still.
Only the thorn tree swayed slightly in the breeze,
And then a flute-like note floated out
Upon the wondering air:
"Oh! my little blue-jay, my little bluebell,
I would I could come to thee;

I would find all the food for thy sin-stained brood,
And thy bridegroom I should be.
That villainous fop on the old beech limb
And the arrogant wife that sits by him
Have broken the heart of my little bluebell,
The little gazelle, the bird gazelle he loved so well,
And they laugh in their cynical glee.
Oh! I would heal thy deep chagrin,
Forgive thy blood-stained life its sin,
And thou shouldst be my beauteous bride,
Forever happy at my side.
My hope, my joy, my love, my pride,
If I could only come to thee,
If I could only come to thee."

Again the air was silent as the tomb.
The little mother bird
Moved with her frightened children
Toward the old thorn tree.
And when she at last stood
Beneath the sword
Upon which her faithful lover was pinioned
Behold the miracle that was enacted
Before her wondering eyes.
The crimson dyes
That streaked the birdlings' wings and breasts
Turned suddenly to a dull and dark maroon,
And not a jay in all birdland
But would swear that her little children
Now resembled in every line and stain
The dead body of her valiant lover
Who had shed his blood
To save his little bluebell from betrayal.

Lector House believes that a society develops through a two-fold approach of continuous learning and adaptation, which is derived from the study of classic literary works spread across the historic timeline of literature records. Therefore, we aim at reviving, repairing and redeveloping all those inaccessible or damaged but historically as well as culturally important literature across subjects so that the future generations may have an opportunity to study and learn from past works to embark upon a journey of creating a better future.

This book is a result of an effort made by Lector House towards making a contribution to the preservation and repair of original ancient works which might hold historical significance to the approach of continuous learning across subjects.

HAPPY READING & LEARNING!

LECTOR HOUSE LLP
E-MAIL: lectorpublishing@gmail.com

9 789354 206610